Children's Authors

R. L. Stine

Cari Meister
ABDO Publishing Company

visit us at
www.abdopub.com

Published by ABDO Publishing Company, 4940 Viking Drive, Suite 622, Edina, Minnesota 55435. Copyright © 2001 Abdo Consulting Group, Inc., Pentagon Tower, P.O. Box 36036, Minneapolis, Minnesota 55435 USA. International copyrights reserved in all countries. No part of this book may be reproduced in any form without written permission from the publisher.

Printed in the United States.

Photos: AP/Wide World, Ohio State University Archives, Corbis, Nickelodeon
Editors: Tamara L. Britton, Christine Fournier, Kate A. Furlong
Art Direction: Pat Laurel, Neil Klinepier

Library of Congress Cataloging-in-Publication Data

Meister, Cari.
    R. L. Stine / Cari Meister
      p. cm.
    Includes index.
    ISBN 1-57765-484-6
    1. Stine, R. L.--Juvenile literature. 2. Young adult fiction--Authorship--Juvenile literature.
3. Authors, American--20th century--Biography--Juvenile literature. 4. Horror tales--Authorship
--Juvenile literature. [1. Stine, R. L. 2. Authors, American.] I. Title.

PS3569.T4837 Z78 2001
813'.54--dc21

                                               00-049603

Contents

R. L. Stine

*R*obert Lawrence Stine was born in Columbus, Ohio. Everybody called him Bob. As a child, he liked to read books and magazines. Soon he began to write his own.

Bob wrote all through school. In college, he worked on *Sundial*, the school's humor magazine. He dreamed of moving to New York City and creating a humor magazine of his own.

After college, Bob taught school for a year. Then he moved to New York. He had several writing jobs. Finally, he got a job where he could create his own humor magazine.

Soon, Bob wrote a humorous book. He eventually wrote many funny books. Then an **editor** asked him to write a scary book.

Bob wrote several scary books before he got the idea for the Fear Street book series. Readers loved the Fear Street series. It became the most popular book series in the U.S.

Then Bob created a series of scary books for younger readers. It was called Goosebumps. It was a popular series, too. Goosebumps was made into a TV program.

Today Bob receives about 500 fan letters a week. And he has created a new series called Nightmare Room. Bob loves to write scary books. And readers love what he writes.

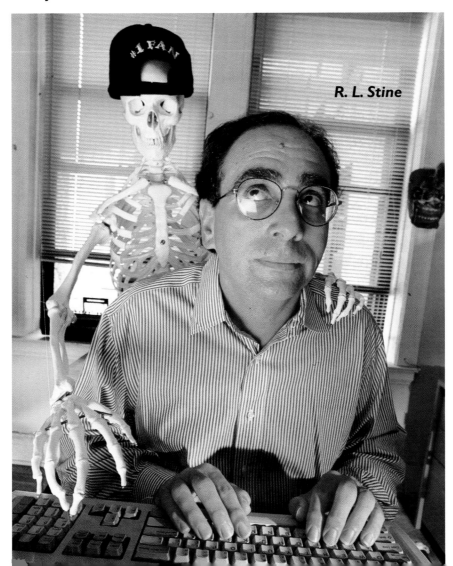

R. L. Stine

Growing up in Ohio

Bob was born on October 8, 1943, in Columbus, Ohio. He was the first child of Lewis and Anne Stine. Bob had a younger brother and sister, Bill and Pam.

Bob lived with his family in a small brick house in Bexley, Ohio. He shared a bedroom with Bill. At night, Bob and Bill told each other bedtime stories. Bob often told scary stories. The stories gave Bill goosebumps.

Sometimes Bob stopped telling the story during an exciting part. Bill would beg to know the story's ending. But Bob would not tell him. He liked to leave Bill guessing.

Bob liked to read. His favorite stories were fairy tales, Greek myths, and Norse **legends**. Bob also liked to listen to the radio. He particularly liked mystery shows like *The Shadow* and *Suspense*. His favorite radio shows were **broadcast** from New York City. Bob dreamed about moving to New York some day.

But Bob was not an adventurous kid. For example, at summer camp, Bob couldn't jump into the pool. He was too scared.

When Bob was seven, his family had to move into a smaller house. Before he moved, Bob wanted to explore the attic. His mother had warned him never to go up there. But one day, Bob sneaked up into the attic. He found something that changed his life. He found a **portable** typewriter.

Bob poses with the plastic skeleton that keeps him company while he writes.

Reading & Writing

*B*ob loved to read funny comic books like *Mad* magazine. He also liked scary comics. Two of his favorites were *Tales from the Crypt* and *Vault of Horror*. Now that he had a typewriter, Bob could make his own magazines.

His first magazine was *The All New Bob Stine Giggle Book.* It was filled with jokes. The magazine was only three inches by four inches (8 cm by 10 cm). And Bob only typed on the front side of the pages.

In 1956, Bob wrote *Hah, For Maniacs Only!!* In this magazine, Bob made fun of popular television shows. This is called **satire**.

In junior high school, Bob started a new satire magazine. It was called *From Here to Insanity*. Bob's magazines were getting better. His sense of satire and humor was improving. And he was typing on both sides of the paper.

Just before Bob's thirteenth birthday, he was preparing for his **bar mitzvah**. His mother interrupted and asked what he would like for a gift. He asked for a new typewriter. Bob's parents supported his ambition to be a writer. So they gave him a big, sturdy office typewriter!

In high school, Bob began his first **novel**. It was called *Lovable Bear*. He also read a lot. He especially liked books by Isaac Asimov, Ray Bradbury, and Robert Sheckley.

In 1961, Bob graduated from high school. That fall, he entered Ohio State University (OSU).

Mad, Tales from the Crypt, *and* **Vault of Horror** *were some of Bob's favorite comics.*

Jovial Bob Stine

Bob was excited about attending OSU. He wanted to write for *Sundial*. It was the school's humor magazine. The magazine was filled with practical jokes, funny stories, and **campus** news.

Bob spent most of his time working on *Sundial*. During his **sophomore** year, Bob became *Sundial's* **editor**. Sometimes he wrote every story in the magazine. Because he was so funny, Bob became known as **Jovial** Bob Stine.

During his senior year, Bob ran for student council president as a joke. He wouldn't be at OSU to serve as president since he was graduating. He just wanted to see how many votes he could get. He lost the election. But he got 1,163 votes!

Bob graduated from college in 1965. His dream was still to move to New York City. But he didn't have enough money. So Bob got a job as a substitute teacher. Then, he taught history for a year.

When he had enough money saved, Bob left teaching and headed for New York.

*Bob with extra copies of **Sundial***

Off to New York!

Bob arrived in New York City in 1966. He loved the city right away. There were lots of bookstores. Some even stayed open all night!

During his first year in New York, Bob had several jobs. He wrote **interviews** with famous people for a teen fan magazine. But he never spoke with the **celebrities**. His boss told him to make up the stories!

Bob lost his job with the fan magazine when the company went out of business. Then he worked as a writer for a magazine called *Soft Drink Industry*.

Bob liked working as a writer. But he didn't want to write about soda pop. So he went to school at New York University. He also looked for a new job during his lunch hour.

During this time Bob met Jane Waldhorn at a party. They liked each other and began to date.

In 1968, Bob got a job with Scholastic, Inc. He wrote articles for *Junior Scholastic* magazine. On June 22, 1969, Bob and Jane got married.

Then in 1972, Bob worked on a magazine called *Search*. It taught social studies to kids in a fun way. But his favorite magazine was one he created called *Bananas*. It was a funny magazine with comics and jokes like *Sundial*.

Bob liked his job at Scholastic. He learned to write fast. He usually worked on four different issues at once!

New York City

A Funny Start

*O*ne day when Bob was working at Scholastic, he got a phone call. It was from a children's book **editor** named Ellen Rudin. She worked at a publishing house called E. P. Dutton. Rudin liked Bob's work on *Bananas*. She asked Bob to write a funny book for kids. Bob's first book was called *How to be Funny*. E. P. Dutton published it in 1978.

How to be Funny was a guidebook. It had tips on how to be funny at the dinner table, at school, or at parties.

Then Bob created another humor magazine for Scholastic called *Maniac*. And in 1980, his son Matthew was born. But five years later, Scholastic couldn't afford to make *Maniac* anymore. They had to fire Bob.

Bob was out of a job. But he didn't mind. Now he had more time to write books. He wrote over 25 funny books under his college nickname, **Jovial** Bob Stine.

Opposite page:
An issue of **Bananas** *magazine*

seventeen

BANANAS

CHERYL LADD
The Human Angel

Moving to Fear Street

When he was not writing funny books, Bob worked on other projects. He wrote bubble gum cards, adventure **novels**, coloring books, and joke books.

In 1983, Bob's wife Jane and her friend Joan Waricha started a company called Parachute Press. The company **packaged** books.

Bob continued to write. He wrote scripts for *Eureeka's Castle*, a puppet show on Nickelodeon. After its first season, it won a CableACE award for best children's show.

Then Jean Feiwel of Scholastic asked Bob to write a horror novel. Bob had always liked scary comic books, movies, and stories. But he had never thought about writing scary books.

But Bob could not say no. He agreed to write a book called *Blind Date*. It was published in 1986. The book was an instant best-seller. Bob knew what it was like to be scared after his experience with the pool at camp. He used these feelings to write stories that would scare others.

Bob began to write other scary books. He started writing the Fear Street series in 1989. His wife's company **packaged** the books.

Fear Street books were horror **novels** for kids aged 9 to 14. The books were connected by their **setting**. Nearly all the characters lived on Fear Street. All of Bob's experience writing quickly for magazines paid off. He wrote a book a month. Fear Street soon became the most popular book series in the U.S.

The characters of Eureeka's Castle

Goosebumps

One day Joan Waricha suggested that Bob write a series of scary books for younger readers. The first Goosebumps book arrived in bookstores in 1992. It was called *Welcome to Dead House.* Children loved it!

Goosebumps books are for children aged 8 to 12. They're just as exciting as the Fear Street books, but not as scary.

Each chapter in a Goosebumps book has a cliff-hanger ending. This is the same trick Bob used on his brother Bill when he told stories at bedtime. Readers just can't wait to find out what will happen next. This is called **suspense**.

Bob gets ideas for his books from his imagination and his experiences. The idea for *The Haunted Mask* came from his son. One Halloween, Matt put on a mask. But he couldn't pull it off. Bob didn't help Matt get the mask off. Instead he ran to his computer to jot down some ideas!

Goosebumps is one of the most popular book series of all time. In 1995, it was made into a TV series on Fox Kids network. Bob likes to watch his stories on TV. Sometimes, he goes to the set where they are filmed.

*Bob sits with masks from the **Goosebumps** television series.*

Fame & Fortune

Several of Bob's books have won the Children's Choice Award from the American Library Association. The Goosebumps series is listed in *Guinness World Records 2000* as the world's top-selling children's book series. Today, more than 300 million copies of Bob's books have been sold.

Bob writes 15 to 20 pages a day, six days a week. Each year, he writes 24 books. And he doesn't plan on stopping anytime soon.

In August 2000, Bob started a new series of books called the Nightmare Room. In this series, the characters appear to live in a normal world. But they're actually in the Nightmare Room, where anything could happen.

Though he is famous, Bob is a regular guy. He likes to spend time with his son. He likes to read and play pinball. He even has his own pinball machine in his apartment. And he loves to write scary stories.

Opposite page: Bob soon after HarperCollins
published the first Nightmare Room book

21

Glossary

bar mitzvah - a ceremony for Jewish boys who, at age 13, take on personal and religious responsibilities. To prepare for the ceremony, boys memorize songs and prayers that they recite during Sabbath-day worship services.

broadcast - to send out information.

campus - the grounds and buildings of a university, college, or school.

celebrity - a famous person.

editor - a person who makes sure a piece of writing has no errors before it is published.

interview - a meeting at which one person gains information from another.

jovial - of good humor.

legend - a story handed down from the past that many people believe is true, but that can't be proven.

novel - a long book, usually about human experience.

package - to prepare books to be published by a publishing company.

portable - able to be carried or moved around.

satire - writing that makes fun of qualities of human life.

setting - the place where a story happens.

sophomore - a student in the second year of high school or college.

suspense - excitement in waiting for a decision or outcome.

Internet Sites

The Official Goosebumps Site

http://place.scholastic.com/goosebumps/high/stine/index.htm

Check out "What's Ghouly this Month," or go to the "Field of Screams" for some scary adventures, games, and jokes. You can also read more about R. L. Stine, find his latest books, and order Goosebumps gear.

The Official Nightmare Room Site

http://www.thenightmareroom.com

Enter at your own risk! Check out clips from R. L. Stine's latest Nightmare Room books. Read an exclusive online story, share your nightmares on the message board, and send an e-card to a friend!

Index